MW00701016

THE SLOW ART

THE SLOW ART

SIERRA GOLDEN

BEAR STAR PRESS

COHASSET, CALIFORNIA

Queries about the use of the poems in this book
may be directed to the editor.

BEAR STAR PRESS
185 HOLLOW OAK DRIVE
COHASSET, CA 95973
530.891.0360 /onemillionbears@gmail.com

COVER ART: COREY ARNOLD / COREYFISHES.COM
AUTHOR PHOTO: SHELLEY GOLDSTEIN
COVER DESIGN: SIERRA GOLDEN
BOOK DESIGN: BETH SPENCER
KNOTS: PROJECT GUTENBERG
FISHERMAN'S
CLOVE HITCH
WEAVER'S
GARRICK BEND

The publisher would like to thank Dorothy Brunsman
for her support of the press from its inception.

for Pop

Contents

I

II

III

Stranger, come sit with me under the madrone.
I have heard the whales sighing all night,
their breath rasping like sandpaper. The leaves
have fallen, again.

This place beside me,

perhaps it is yours?

APPETITE

In the gravel parking lot
behind the blue laundromat
I find raspberries, though here
in the rain arched canes are rare.

Haven't been on land in weeks—
it seems everything could knock
me over. The steam stack leaks
the smell of fish rot and bleach.

I find the exact wood screws
I need in the hardware store.
There's fresh water, hot showers,
clothes warm out of the dryer,

a bar full of strangers, cell
service, and this berry patch
where feral plants have blossomed
and bear tiny chartreuse fruit.

I want to eat each one. I
want to walk back to the boat,
cupping the whole harvest, leave
nothing for the rest of town.

Imagining the berries
roe-colored, I see, somehow,
salmon thrashing in black nets.
Berry-pink pearls spawned on deck.

Each day someone does something
worse to another so what
would it matter if I ate
all the raspberries alone?

What could possibly happen
if I placed each in the palm
of another—one for her,
for him, for them, for me, for you?

GRUB

That's my dad, he said, and I watched
the practiced pair box groceries. Only market
in town, unless you count the liquor store
across the street from the laundromat
where fishermen collect to gossip and swap
dirty magazines while smoking and soaking
the scent of fish from their lucky pair of sweats.
The kid ran the register and slid milk, eggs,
whatever couldn't keep long on the boat,
down the counter, stopped to help with boxes
when his dad fell behind trying to Sharpie cardboard
for dockside delivery, heap of groceries piled
before him. He asked, *How do you spell 'Challenger'?*
I take the word for granted. The boy must too,
though he spells it aloud for his father.
It was graceful and sad that summer, watching
salmon die in the same stream where they hatched.
Their bodies we call ghost fish might swim for days,
hollow as zombies the man and boy watch on TV at dusk.

GRACIAS

Cannery workers greet us by the ice chute
and splash into the hold, shimmering
water thigh-high and thirty-four degrees.
They pump it dry. Frayed tie-ups loop
around tar-blacked pilings. Sway-backed
dock creaks high above our gray mast
at low tide. Wet snow clumps down.
Someone hums "You Are My Sunshine"
as clouds sink over the dock. Lights flick on
before sunset, fight the damp and dark.
Jorge and Gordo off-load sixty tons of herring.
Their heaving lungs hang steam puffs
big as buoys in the ripe roe smell of the hold.
They shuffle and shovel the gape-mouthed fish.
A cork-yellow moon cracks cloud cover,
and shrouds us all in the same half-shadow.
I wish on milky scales stuck like stars
to their neoprene green pants
that I never have to leave here, never
have to weave a home in some far-flung place,
dreaming my family together while
I work a job no one wants.

ROSE'S

Rose's is empty these days,
old oak bar smoke-stained and carved
all over with varnished names
and spidering cracks like scars.

Fake and fading roses wilt
on the untuned piano
where I learned to play "Chopsticks"
and Chopin, sang soprano

for fishermen and cannery
workers after my bedtime.
Mother, holding a lime, would
scold me, head shaking, then mime

"just one more" over the crowd.
Men, rowdy, yelling for beer
would grin, call me dear, and leave
a coin or two heaped up here

on the piano bench. I'd
hide them in my small pink heart-
purse, sneaking one at a time,
making the big pile look sparse.

I'd dream of a real stage, save
all the sticky change, count it
each night, wondering how much
was enough for red velvet

curtains, but I found fast boys,
big joints. The slick money ran
through my fingers like dust motes
drifting in the piano's

strings. When the snow fell, I wrote
my first love note, sipping hot
toddies by the pot-belly stove.
I overflowed my heart, sought

love in a snowman's cold kiss.
Skunk cabbage unfurled, black bears
nipping them off near the mist-
drenched ground. In the first bad year,

the cannery closed, but boats
would float in anyway. Night
after night, skippers sat moored
on tall red stools till daylight.

I learned to slosh out whiskey
and gin, fry crisp fish and chips,
but each summer I pour less
liquor, count more empty slips.

The last folks—famous Rose too
(my tough, bucktoothed, bartending
mom)—have gone away, will soon
pass away. I wince and bend,

pull a small string. The hot pink
tubes and links of neon light
flicker, fight shadows, and then,
are wrenched into the sinking night.

LEFTOVERS

In the red
rust of morning,
a salmon fisherman

mends his seine,
hardening his hands
stitch by stitch.

In the galley, the cook
scrambles eggs, tosses
the shells to a rising tide.

A circling hummingbird
touches its slender
beak to the trash.

The skipper's kids
hide and seek behind
a stack of crab pots,

and the shipwright urges
boat-work, new caulking
with pine-soaked oakum.

A wet mop slops
across the sky, and
the rain begins again.

At dinnertime,
the harbormaster meets
a boat by the crooked pier,

she and the evergreen
trees dripping
in the gathering dark

while her family says grace
around a yellow cedar table
with their eyes closed.

FOUNDATION

This winter, I live in a shed
because the county says it is
too small to be a house.
                        What
do they know of a home?

HOUSEWARMING

The day I move, shuffling boxes and baggage
from car to porch, porch to door, door to loft,
Amos spends helping friends slaughter pigs,
shots echoing from the neighbor's orchard,
scent of apples rotting in the sun mingling
with steaming blood. That night, he brings
me a heart in white butcher paper. Together
we unwrap the rust-colored lump, wondering
which knife, how sharp, where do we slice?
What can we savor, and what, if anything,
should we throw to the dogs?

Net Work

Shuttles flick through diamond-shaped windows.
Fingers flash, bend twine in stair steps
up and down cut edges. Their pockets full of hooks
and flagging tape, men mend the net.

Jim recalls branding cattle as a kid in North Dakota,
winter cold just lifted, calves struggling in mud
before the prairie bloomed, withered in summer heat.
Playing cowboy now, he says he shot coyotes
and thieves off his dad's land. You only know

he's fibbing when his fingers stutter, the tiny knot
coming up slack. Just one unraveled compromises
the delicate lift and pull of meshes under stress.
He's seen whole seams split from end to end,

knows love knots pull tighter under pressure, stronger
than the lines used to tie them, and starts talking
about his grandmother with Alzheimer's. Each winter
she thinks every day for a week is Christmas.
Last year she fell in two feet of snow.

Feeding the horses, hay in her hands, the wind at ten
below, she lay crying until Jim's grandfather found her.
She didn't recognize him, but knew love
when it grabbed her, pushing back the terror.

Jim joins two lines with overhand knots, sliding them
one on top of the other, pulling for tension.
Sometimes the line snaps in his swollen fingers.
His hands ache. He cracks his knuckles, asks the boys
if they're ready for a beer, remembering his first:

at fifteen he drank Rainier, the bittersweet scent
biting his nose while he sipped, making him crave pancakes.
He didn't know why until he remembered hunting trips
when he was young and Hot Betty, the old flattop stove

at his uncle's cabin where Jim's dad would tinker
the diesel flame into smothering heat, sizzle of bacon
while Uncle Joe poured Hamm's in the pancake batter,
saying, *Our little secret.* Holding a burnt-handled spatula,
he'd flip white beer cakes mid-air.

Outside the web locker, Jim's crew chuckles,
calls it a day, each man popping a beer tab.
At home their fingers twitch all night, tie imaginary
hitches, sheet bends, loop knots, a bowline on a bight.
Jim dreams of the whole net flexing, all the pearl-sized
knots shrunk and snug, rippling in the current.

TOWN DAY

They say the dump, a mile outside town, is the only place with cell service.

And so he clomps off the boat
and off the float, up the ramp,
away from town, hot showers,
a fresh bag of flour, and stamps

for stacks of love notes he wrote
on watch ignoring the whales.
He turns left at the king hung
from a ladder's rung, gills veiled

with blood, and puddled red guts
saved for dogs baying under
the boardwalk. Quick sounds of town
give out to the woods and dump.

There's no silence. It's all breeze,
spruce trees whiskering his ears,
and eldritch calls of ravens
scavenging bones and beer cans.

Today's the day he finally
gets to call his one sweetheart.
All that time fishing, nothing
but Skipper's grunts cut the hard

face of solitude. Ten days
waiting for invisible
waves to carry his tin voice
across vast land, across dull,

plain houses huddled in clumps,
and into cold plastic pressed
to the precious ear his tongue
loves to enter, caressing

calyx-whorls of cartilage
and tender folds of pink flesh.
And so he lingers all day
at the dump. He dials and dials,

fingers moving like pretty
please, like knock on wood, like long
prayers, like rain dancers bright
in his loneliness who stomp

for a connection that comes
on just the right wind above
the tattered trash. It does what
it can to keep them in love.

Long Distance

Summer you go
deckload the boat
alone, stack fish
like wood, silver
cord we live by
all winter.

We'll pass one
mug between us,
sitting by the fire
you light.

I'll pass
the postcards
you wrote
between us
too.

How lovely
we'll say,
how lonely,
to be apart
and in love.

WEATHER REPORT

Sometimes the mist moves
through like a breath. Colors him
foggy. Fills him like a sigh.

Sometimes the mist moves
like breath. Colors him foggy
like a sigh. Sometimes mist

like breath colors him.
Sometimes: Mist. Sigh. Mist.
Sometimes: Sigh. Sigh. Sigh.

THE VIEW

Morning, and the rosehips stay plump with frost
then pucker and thaw in sea breeze from the bluff.
Two figures hold hands and traverse the mud,
their outlines small against the shattered clouds,
the wind shipping whole fragments to my shed.
From bed, I hear: *bowerbird... blossom... bounty.*
All the beautiful Bs thump as shutting doors do.
I hear: *Listen, darling...* I hear: *Lousy you...*
I think: *Language is smaller than love, is a nest*
when a spaceship is needed.

BED BUGS

The boat, full hold,
runs in deep cold.
In dusk's fo'c'sle
we crewmen wear

sheer sleep and hear
snores. Dream of beer,
the slightest fear
of dawn the work

day brings, its jerk
hard. This murky
night, Skipper skirts
Olalla Point,

rubs swollen joints
and lucky coins,
wants to anoint
the autumn's plum-

dark with light rum,
chooses milk, hums,
broods as it un-
ravels white threads

in coffee. In bed
we sleep, bugs feed,
skitter on heads,
hands, hearts, and sink

torch tongues in skin
glass smooth and thin.
Little beasts, pin
puncture mouths. Ache.

See how we wake
naked, how we find
the smallest butcher
making of us meat.

PREDAWN

She used to sleep through the night,
stretched long and thin down the narrow bunk,
but year after year, she sleeps less,
learning the sounds of a creaking vessel.
An old friend groaning, its planks moan
and its engine whistles high all night.
She trusts the crew less each day, lies awake
second-guessing their wild turns,
worries about reefs she knows are ahead.
Even her dreams are fat logs
banging the hull and wind
playing the rigging like a broken guitar.
Next to Sisyphus and his rock, she pushes
nightmares up a mountain of water,
while the skipper, her father,
sleeps soundly. She wonders at his faith
in others, the ability to place an entire
life's work in the hands of another.
Maybe it's impossible to pass faith
from father to daughter. She sees only
tiderips, how the worst could capsize a boat.
Cedar ribs would bend and snap, float north
and south. In the frigid water, one body
would be dragged from another.
Her hands would go numb and slip
from the knotted bones of his wrist.

Triangulation

With salmon stacked to the door, she squishes through fish,
boots tracking scales in the wheelhouse, across the galley floor,
down the companionway, and into the engine room.
By the end of the day, scales on the starboard fuel tank,
scales on the mast, deck winch, ladder and steps. Scales
in her hair, in her gloves, up her sleeves, behind her ears.
Scales like freckles. Scales like raindrops. Like bindis,
like dragon skin. Scales in her eyes like contact lenses. Scales
flake. Scales stick fast as glue. Scales flash like diamond chips,
like glow in the dark stars on the ceiling. Fairy dust your first
girlfriend wore on the last day of school. Piñata candy licked
with rust-colored tongues. Scales that taste like caviar,
like salt, like sperm, musty crush of ocean and stink of lust.
These scales. You lucky bastard, you don't even know,
but for each she scrubs and scrapes and cleans away,
she dreams your fingers drumming softly on her skin.
In the shower, she dreams your fingers into streams,
into stars that see, into mist, smoke, fire that breathes.
Your fingers hum whole notes on the bass clef of her back
or sweep window-lips in warm breeze or win fast bets
in a hailstorm of desire. Those fingers smell like diesel,
like danger, like a damp, darling copy of her body. They chart
scars like ocean trenches, flit on her wrist as a seabird skims sky.
They snap buttons on a birthday suit, crank the wrong wrench,
the right wrench, and a screwdriver that turns everything
loose. Fingers like ants, the crumbs they hunt, and sugar
they love. Fingers round as butter, as cream, as you scream
into a cornfield from a car full of flesh. She dreams your fingers
on fleece, on flannel, on copper, on cotton, on nipples,
on knees. How can I compare? I love her the way a king's
black mouth gapes for air, the way any salmon will taste
the whole ocean and still turn for home.

CONVERSATION

In the yard, Amos and I sip tea, talk about love,
seeing and being seen. The living room too
cramped to sit in when the sky unravels so far,
and a stray crocus blooms, and our breaths rise
in puffs between us. Just as I say love is a puddle,
not a cliff, a buck in rut slips through the woods.
Shoulders swollen under a rough coat, his stiff
gait stumbles him so close to us I can see
the glaze of desire in his eyes, and Amos mutters
rifle and buckshot, bending to rise and fetch
them, the deer still for a moment, seeing us
for the first time, as if all of a sudden he knows
just how dangerous love is.

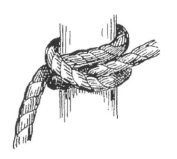

PLAYBOY

Pete's grandfather spent 43 days
lost at sea. Found dead, he held
his cock and a photo of Meemaw.

Now, Meemaw won't let go of Pete's
wrist as he ducks out the door, headed
for the market where nobody minds

if he cops a feel of the peaches.
Later, the hairdresser at Curl Up 'n Dye
fondles his ear lobes, his jaw line,

and some girl on local news escapes
her flaming house because Bobo
the dog dialed 911 with his nose.

The footage shows her rubbing
his jowls as if they might alchemize.
She sobs, *We sleep together every night,*

and with each shot Pete wishes
he were the dog licking her toes,
twisting belly up to be rubbed.

He carries these women with him,
their tongues and cheeks, small
humps of shoulders and knees.

So what? His head rattles with lust.
He's got nothing, and he's asking,
Don't we all burn to be touched?

EXPOSURE

Jesse isn't really a pirate, but the Coast Guard thinks so when he calls to say he found a body. It doesn't matter that she's still alive, so cold she stopped shivering, blue fat of her naked body waxy and blooming red patches where his hands grabbed and hauled her from the water. He stands over her with a filet knife, slowly honing the blade as he waits for Search and Rescue. The glassy eyes of a dead tuna stare up from the galley counter. At dusk, Jesse flicks on the squid lights. When the uniforms arrive, they question Jesse but never tell him who she is. The lifeboat takes her away, its white wake brilliant in the night. Days later, Jesse reads the story of an obese woman slipping out of bed at Johnson Memorial. She shed a hospital-issued flannel gown and left nothing more, not even a whisper of footprints on the white tile floor. Jesse lights up a mass of squid and imagines her bare bottom shining under the moon as she waltzed herself into the slate-gray ocean and floated away. He knows how she must have longed for the cradling dark. He watches ruddy bodies pulse in the artificial bright, the net dropping around them like a curtain.

ROCKFISH

What can I make of this fish, cooked whole,
presented upright on a platter as if swimming
still. Gills, belly, fins wreathed in slivered
peppers and zucchini, sweet peas and peaches.

I've killed a hundred with barbed hooks, stars
strung on a line fine as a spider's, mottled bodies
slick and brilliant plowing up from the dark, bloating,
and breaking the surface. I slung each from the sea,

swim bladder ballooned, stomach protruding
from mouth, black eyes bulging. Their poisonous
spines. Their bony flesh. Their hinged lips. Their anuses
dripping excrement. What can I make of this one?

Only bones remain. Someone not long ago ripped him
from deep water, from the only dark he could bear.

A Kind of Courage

I.

Even after I've slipped my whole hand inside his head,
jerking my arm, index finger curved into cartilage
and bone, the fish's entire weight hanging and dropping,
ripping out feathery, blush-red gills, the king keeps on.

Slit open from anus to chin, guts half gone, the salmon yawns,
gill plate lifting, heart still pumping, shining skin quivering.

II.

My grandmother, living alone—with even a kidney gone—takes me
out for a cheeseburger and Coke. Uncrumpling her last dollar
to tip Steak 'n Shake's bowtied waiters, she tells me
I shouldn't bother coming to her funeral, but when I leave,

she won't let go, folds of her face pressed smooth on my cheek,
her bones fragile, wrist no thicker than a king's caudal bone.

Getting Ready

The mast light flickers furiously, then burns out.
I'm standing there, alone, with my first coffee
and Leonard Cohen, ready for 3 AM watch
after a midnight delivery and all-day fishing.

I want nothing less than to climb the mast,
to fix the light, stubby legs clinging to cold steel,
heart banging as the boat rolls and recovers,
everything humming the same dull vibration,

and so I do nothing, navigating from a pilot chair,
defiant in my shame, sculpting extravagant excuses
from the full moon, the autopilot, the gloriously
dark horizon, not a single ship flaring into sight.

Perhaps the fragile, glowing filament has snapped?
Or the long, coiled wire has burned, the copper
threads singed and frizzed until the light quits?
But surely a short rest is not forbidden.

And so I sit, a splendid ugliness rising inside.
I dread dawn, that hard inescapable light,
the way it heralds the truth.

SHAME

Squirt a soapy spray of Joy
on a rainbow skin of oil
drifting out around the boat.
Shatter the sheen into rough
patches to disguise the mess.
Catch a small salmon—slender
as a runt-of-the-litter
kitten, serrated milk jug
collar cutting his white throat.
Find a beer can in muskeg.
Coors label sun-bleached to bone-
tones in decomposing muck.
Toss another dozen more
over the side, torn in rough
spirals, so they'll sink, shaping
artificial reefs in steep
silvery heaps. Watch bottle caps,
a gas can, paper plates, slice
of saran-wrapped bread come up,
go out with the same net again.
Recover a three-foot wolf eel,
still thrashing in the hold
as it pumps dry, and ignore
his squashed-up, plum-colored
face, ragged grimace frozen
in place, his needle teeth sharp
as shame. Hold a small seabird,
her body the size and weight
of a snowball in your hands.
Fold back her slick black wings broke
by braided mesh and kill her.

Growing Up

Her father taught her to eat sea urchins.
Tapped their dripping purple shells open
with a pocketknife. Slid the gray blade
under a triangle of cognac-colored roe.
The eggs quivered, slipped from the knife
to his tongue. He taught her to dress a trout
in two cuts, to find sea asparagus, forage
for chicken of the woods, salmonberries,
Labrador tea, to light a small fire in the rain.
He taught her to sit quietly, to tell a story,
to listen while he talks about North Dakota,
his father growing wheat, the bite of dust rising
under his feet as a boy, sweet feel of sweat
just before a storm breaks open, first drops
pocking the cracked pond bottom and green
blooms after. She learned about the postcards
her grandfather wrote in the Coast Guard:
Mom, arrived safely in Seattle, though knocked
the top off the mast coming under Ballard Bridge.
Maybe I'll come home when we finish the repairs.
I miss the thunderstorms. It only drizzles here,
and the voice of God is absent from the weather.
How is the garden?

She learned that her dad chipped cement
from bricks for pennies, hoed the weeds
by windbreak-trees and had a pet monkey
named Nola who would spit in your face.
This was before he moved to Alaska, started
fishing for salmon every summer, herring
and halibut in the spring and fall. His first
skipper, a Japanese man called Sneak Attack,
told him urchin shells are five fused plates,

pentamerism that radiates tiny spears weaving
in ocean currents. Sneak taught him to read
a chart and mend the small meshes of a seine
into a perfect pattern of collapsing diamonds.
He drifted by them years ago in Lucky Cove,
her dad nodding *that's him* as he taught her
to run the bilge pump that pushes water
from the belly of the boat through a small hose,
spraying it back into the ocean.

This afternoon a hydraulic hose blew,
pouring fifty gallons of hot yellow slick
all over the engine room. The bilge filled with oil
the color of Dakota wheat her grandfather grew
on the farm, where he later pumped oil
with a hammering black rig. She remembers
learning to play poker on his beige carpet.
The strange way he shuffled, one thumb
shorter than the other, the tip lost long ago.
He sipped whiskey, taught her to bluff and fold,
to go all in with every matchstick she had.

Twelve hours later, there's still oil in the bilge,
stars blaze like a thousand match heads burning,
and their curling wake wavers like blue smoke.
Her dad tells her to pump the muck overboard,
just like he taught her that day in Lucky Cove.
She's told to do it in the dark, middle of her midnight
watch. Then he sleeps while she dims
the deck lights too low for another boat to spot.
She turns the yellow handle, checks over the rail
to see water pour from the bilge hose.
The white gush turns to the slow slop of oil,
morphing grey shapes eerie in Icy Strait.
All she can think of are the sea urchins,
how she's read that tube feet push their globes
along stacks of sea rocks the same blue-black color

as the Coast Guard uniform her grandfather left her.
It fits like it was tailored in Japan for her and not him.
At eighteen he was a small man.

When her dad was eighteen, he left home
and everything her grandfather ever wanted
to teach him. Taste of whiskey, the good burn
in his throat. How to grow blond wheat that rolls
like waves. That business of the ground spilling
black gold like blood, as if bitten by a sea urchin's
five self-sharpening teeth. They cut through stone.
The mouth, Aristotle wrote, looks like a horn lantern.
Or he didn't. Everyone disagrees how to translate
which parts of urchins he penned into light,
so she doesn't know whether to imagine the mouth
as a beacon inside, or not.

She wants something of her own to light a path,
to flicker like a small oil lamp in the dark.
Instead, she's got smudge of oil and smoke
staining her fingers the same as her grandfather
stained his, pulling oil in streams from the earth.
She's dumping it back, watching it seep and spread.
Her father doesn't know what he's asked.
Under the boat's greasy sheen sea urchins chew
through micro-algae, seaweed, fish carcasses,
even another urchin's fingerling spines.
Clouds cover pinprick stars. It begins to rain.
There is no light. She turns the yellow handle back,
the slow slop stops. She finishes her shift at the wheel,
sleeps in her bunk at sunup. Curtains pulled
against the light, she dreams the whole mess again
and again, trying to teach herself how to be
her father's daughter, how to let her grandfather's
black ashes blow back into the prairie.

Under the Madrone

The stranger said: *Love is a vice, almost*
tight as tentacles, the weight of a blue whale.
It's work beyond the shape of my hands.

I want love to be a featherweight,
wish I could dovetail my words with but.
I would say but this error is the sign of love,

but not even the rain has such small hands,
but my sweetheart and I are a body
I will not dismantle bone by bone.

I said: *Last night, I walked by the neighbor's*
boat—a skeleton waiting for skin—
in a rundown shed lit from within.

The shipwright had lugged a steam box into place,
planed luminous broad beams, and laid the keel
like a spine. He knows what you don't:

the slow art of bending ribs. To find
the breaking point night after night.
To stop short.

THE SONG OF A BOAT

I first saw you
in the bucket-dark
dusk, a season
of half-bit snow, you
dressed in a shawl of it.
Frozen lines creaked
on cleats and then
when spring climbed into
summer, I opened
your doors, tamped oakum
into invisible seams,
stoked the diesel stove,
stripped you
to bone-colored planks.
I brushed gloss back
into wood steamed
till it bent, curved into
the song of a boat.

Salmon rang
in the sound like bells
we answered. What else
could we do,
the years going by
while town discovered
knick-knacks and meth?

All those days
I fished. I looked through
your rigging
to the ocean below
and the night
and you were the way
in the dark I could see.

At Midnight without a Moon

he died, and his daughter was seized by a great curiosity
about what it was like for him, delusional on his death bed,
seeing great schools of salmon, calling out:

Set the net, set the net!
Was this the soul returning to his body for a last trip?
She would have fished his boat, but it had been sold.

She wondered if a soul could leave a living body.
If so, where his had gone the last years, him living
so far from the water, his body landsick.

Those years after the boat returned to port,
the kettle singing *wakeup, wakeup* a last time,
she wrung the salt and breeze from his hair,

and sluiced the smell of sea and diesel from his hands,
torso, and thighs. She washed his whole body,
asking herself what, if any, ecstatic light remained.

PLEASURE

After a good soak I stand
at the top of the trail,

sockless in my Xtratufs and sweats,
nipples and knees stuck to the pilly cotton.

I pluck salmonberries one after another
into the upturned bowl of my shirt.

A warm summer drizzle begins,
and everything turns to mud.

I watch it squish up the sides of my boots,
watch the drops pock my gray shirt,

and with stained, wrinkled fingers,
twist the hair clinging to my cheeks.

They say that bears can smell
berries and blood from miles away.

I wouldn't hear his padded feet
brushing down from the muskeg,

his matted fur snagging pine needles and twigs,
or see his snotted nose among the new leaves.

How strange it would be to know
he could devour a small stag

after watching his pink tongue stretch
and curl around a tiny red berry in the rain.

Carved on the Docks

Weathered cedar creaks beneath my feet
while I roam from boat to boat
and the edge of a storm begins to blow.
Chips and splinters fly, split by an axe
that creaks in meter (swish, chunk, swish, chunk)
peeling away one face to reveal another.
Ravaged bark to smooth high forehead,
grim brows, vacant blue eyes, proud arching nose,
and fat red lips, a mask to be hung in a stranger's home
marked with the sweet smell of browning bread
or the long burn of savage quips, lashed
from heart to heart. He sees through me.
Surprising how even this intimacy hurts.

ASH AND WARM AIR

Blacktail deer graze, shoulders and backs slacked
and relaxed, only their ears still tense, listening
for anything. Cracking or singing makes tails
flick and whole bodies rise over the fence
like woodstove smoke disappearing in the night.
This morning is the color and texture of smoke,
frost-white grass, and light sifting through
lifting fog. The alder logs Amos split are burnt
to ash and warm air already risen past the rafters.
Under thin blankets, we spoon. In the chill,
we watch does chew, their wet noses wrinkling,
the first bit of heat kindling between us.

Not Fishing

One of the best things about fishing is not fishing.
   —Hollis Jennings, commercial fishing boat captain

I don't want to know
the way snow dissolves,
falling into saltwater,

the way solstice light
begins to creep back
into mornings on watch,

the way hands
cramp baiting hooks
one after another

while stars shine
like spilt salt
on the black bread of night.

I don't want to know
the VHF sputtering sweet nothings
on Valentine's day,

though I do know
the small stones
I carry in my heart.

I don't want to know
the weight of a winter king,
his body thrashing

on the side of the boat,
streaming bloody
water and wrack,

his black mouth
yawning with want,
yellow eyes wide as a child's.

I never want to leave
home in winter
to fish.

I want to trade
the ocean
for a cup of tea,

an arm
around my waist,
the small mercies of home.

FLIGHT

Ground too wet for snow to stick, wind puffing
just so, white flakes fall up. I fake-read Blake
and wait, watching dark hover in raccoon-gray
clouds, the dampness running a cold snout
across my knuckles and toes. When the night
has stuck for sure, the flurries stick too. I start
cooking, and Amos pauses outside the lit
kitchen, watches me sift flour in small drifts.
I cut it with butter, roll out small balls of dough.
I can feel him fold the whole scene into a
paper spaceship and flip it into flight.

Winter Heat

Months after the neighbors piled their firewood
tall as the windows, wide as the house, and strung
brown plastic between the pine trees, protecting
their winter heat and blocking my view,

it snows, and in the morning, the tarp-tented
heaps of uncut logs appear suddenly beautiful.
Just a fine shake of flakes shining in the sun,
tree-drips pattering on plastic, and I am in love

for a moment, thinking, *Is this how a poem happens?*
One day I sit in bed past any reasonable hour,
and finally stop thinking about the neighbors
stealing my view, about everything needing doing

or undoing: the dishes, my taxes, the mess I made
with my exes. Seeing the sap-leaking stacks of wood
as if for the first time, some part of me collapses—
maybe my work ethic? Personal aesthetics?

Moral standards? Whatever it was, wherever it stood
inside me opens, letting in what little light there is.

BATHHOUSE

The kids can remember to call me Fish Doctor,
but two weeks in, most of the locals still say hey
stranger, out-of-towner, what's-her-face.

Nobody remembers biologist, visiting scientist,
and especially not ichthyologist. I dropped in
on a roadless town. Nobody showers at home,

washing instead in pairs, small groups of the same sex
soaking in sulphur-scented water between gashed-out
rocks and concrete tucked in a tiny clapboard house.

Sign says clothing not optional, women welcome
during men's hours, men never welcome during women's.
How intimately the people of this small town must know each other.

My first bath, women creased open like old letters
soap, slather, and chatter, tease me until I peel down forbidden
bikini strings inch-worming across my thighs and neck.

A little lumpy lady with hair like kelp tells me to rinse
in the corner, explains the name Dickel Gang. I was lost
in the story, but I loved the way fat crackled her memory.

We lived in a tent, she said, and John shot a black bear
snuffling at the canvas door. Friends came from all over
the island to eat roasted bear. The whole gang sipped Dickel,

watched the carcass sizzle and spit over coals the color of salmon roe
while the flagrant scent of lard stooped into their stomachs.
I told her about researching octopuses with their three hearts, armored

sculpin, and hagfish escaping death in a blossom of slime.
We both knew starry flounders, white bellies of pink salmon,
and opalescent roe of herring. Sometimes, I said, it seems

I live among the fish, their smooth flat bodies gliding silently past
in the gloom. Someone sang out and soon all the mouths opened.
Bawdy buoyant songs rose from the women's lungs.

I could not join, only study them, mottled, dimpled, delighted,
unlike any fish I know, except maybe halibut, holy ones
spawning at the brink of a continental shelf. What faith!
It holds them together at the edge of a bottomless dark.

Independence Day at Rose's

The poster reads: Teeny-Weenie Contest.
I tack it on top of ragged old fliers, corners flapping
in a stiff breeze. This one is glossy, bright as tin cans

or copper penny nails at the local hardware.
Covered in red, white, and blue stars,
it's "the big deal" around this fish-town, so don't go

thinking dirty thoughts. It's all fun and games
and, truth be told, the Fourth of July needs every teeny-weenie
bit of excitement teeny-peenies can muster up.

"Dying Town Loves Sex" headlines the paper next island over;
that tourist-trap of Princess Cruise Line jewelry stores
likes to joke our top prize is the biggest truck in town,

but here is just a boardwalk row of shanties built on stilts
above the tide. Not a single road. We just want to see the little guy
a big winner for once.

COLD NIGHTS

Fire unlit, I slide small blades through fresh herring, thin ribs just a prickle as they crack, flesh peeling into strips no longer or thicker than my palm. Breath shivering out, shadows scooping into a small circle of light, you layer mason jars with onions, lemons, fragile white fillets, and the bitter embrace of pickle juice cooled in the dark. Pink peppercorns drift like planets. Cloves comets. These cold nights, the jar is the universe and we find its light.

ELEGY

For breakfast, I eat the sticky rolls you made and think of riding
in the fields. You always clipped the gates shut behind us,
keeping the cows in their place. We never knew

when they were going to take off down the highway, trotting,
irretrievable, dropping slick pies on the pavement, hazards
for the drivers just shifting up as they crested the bluff.

Here's to the cows, then, milling loosely along the fence.
To the heifer with a white face and one blue eye.
She drops her weight from hoof to hoof,

tail impatient, flicking the flies. Here's to the rotting,
to the silt on your best boots, to the glassy look
your eyes took the last years.

You died in August. Summer harvest just beginning
when you were here, kneading sweet cinnamon dough
while burrs caught in the dog's fur.

I was not here—two thousand miles away—spilling fish
from a seine net. I didn't even think of you, except to wonder
if you'd make it through the summer. I had my own problems.

The crewman sipping gin hidden in the baking bin.
The skiff billowing black smoke so thick it looked as if God
were smudging it off the water with a stick of charcoal.

I'm here now, in time for the memorial, sitting
where you sat, drinking the coffee you bought,
the sticky rolls not even stale.

The neighbors planted 100 acres of sunflowers
but you knew that, having watched the tractors sow seed
and having seen the sprouts shine argentine with dew.

There is no dew now. The heat too dry. The shoots rigid stalks,
the blossoms about to be cut. How could I have missed it?
All this scrutiny and I miss the obvious, ordinary, stupendous

eternity of love. It's as if you were still here,
as if you will wake in the chair patched with a plaid blanket
where the dog chewed a hole in the upholstery.

As if you will look out the window and say again
how beautiful the sunflowers are. Here's to you.
Look, you would say, look how they tilt into the light.

THE SOUND OF OARS

To hear the faint sound of oars in the silence as a rowboat
comes slowly out and then goes back is truly worth
all the years of sorrow that are to come.
     —Jack Gilbert, "A Brief for the Defense"

I'm here, Jack, like you say, listening to the sound of oars,
dipping and dripping while they pull across the sound,
and, it's true, I'm enjoying my life. At times, I've almost forgotten
the faces of suffering, the flies, but this is not what God wants.
Look, even here, the sheen of oil, a radiant rainbow scar,
and the scent of bleach hovering above a fish creek.
It's the same everywhere: sorrow and slaughter,
the world burning with hopelessness and violence.
Tonight I stand on the bow of a small boat, moored in a tiny port,
the town three shuttered cafes and a bar, shouting and music.
In the morning while sea otters slap through the kelp, feeding,
someone wakes in the street, the neighborhood's curtains clamped
shut. Nobody escapes, but you say *to make injustice*
the only measure of our attention is to praise the Devil.
What then? Your stubborn delight is not enough either.
Even the rockfish migrate, rising from darkness at sunrise,
sinking again in the night.

Meanwhile

The cold settles in,
the kettle whistles,
the honey crystals.
Two cups of tea—
steam!

UNDER THE MADRONE

The stranger asked: *Is my love good?*
He asked me. Has asked others before,
and the truth is I am as lost as him or them,

but I thought: There is a love that is a puddle, not a cliff.
There are people who float you, hold your head
above water, point your eyes to the stars.

These people may or may not be your parents,
your brothers or sisters or cousins. They may be
your lover or teacher. They may be strangers.

They may not ever know how far the strings inside you
unravel when they listen, cracked open, to your story.
Love them anyway as you would like to be loved.

As for the cliff, for a long time I believed it did not exist,
and maybe for some it does not. Maybe
it is more about bodies than I would like to admit.

I thought: Perhaps what I have learned is that somewhere
there is a person who breathes your breath.
This person may be your husband or wife or not.

They may be somewhere near you or in a country
not your own. They may be in your life for a minute
or more. They may make everything inside you shimmer,

and when you fall, you may fly, or float to the sky,
or when you fall, you may find you are falling
to the sea or something harder and stony,

so I said: *If out of all this living, out of all these people,*
Love comes, it will not occur to you to ask
whether it is good.

Salmonberries

The fish plant is closed. The church, empty.
The school. All rotted like raspberries that didn't make it
in the rain anyway. The sun shines today. Once in August.
The post office is open Tuesday and half of Saturday.
The waterline bursts. The café closes. The laundromat too.
Rose's is open, though, her wrinkles gathered up
behind the bar. Whiskey is the only liquor left.
No mixers, no water. The waterline has burst.
Who would want to live here? The residents
proof of something, though, that can't be said
for the town's flickering out, the waiting for only stars
to glow over the belly-burn of booze. We pass
the season's last salmonberries from hand to hand:
one for her, for him, for them, for me, for you.

NOTES

"Leftovers": after Robert Hayden's "Kodachromes of the Island"

"Long Distance": for Brian Hagenbuch

"Triangulation": with an image from Daemond Arrindell

"Playboy": after the photo *Sex on the Beach* taken by Susan A. Barnett

"Exposure": light boats are small fishing boats equipped with several 1,000-watt light bulbs hung from aluminum shades to attract squid to commercial fishing grounds. They are frequently seen on the California coast.

"Growing Up": Aristotle described the chewing organ of sea urchins in his *History of Animals*, and it was long held that he said the chewing organ looked like a horn lantern. This comparison has now been noted as a mistranslation. Aristotle was actually describing the entire body of a sea urchin as looking like a horn lantern. However, in biology, the term "Aristotle's lantern" continues to refer to the chewing organ.

"Under the Madrone": with lines from Lewis Hyde and E. E. Cummings

"The Song of a Boat": after W. S. Merwin's "Elegy for a Walnut Tree"

"At Mightnight without a Moon": after Jack Gilbert and also with much respect for Carley and Lange Solberg

"Bathhouse": with some details from a story heard in the Tenakee Springs bathhouse

"Elegy": after Ellen Bass

"The Sound of Oars": after Jack Gilbert and John Straley

"Meanwhile": after Tod Marshall and Thomas McGrath

"Under the Madrone": after the first letter in Rilke's *Letters to a Young Poet*

ACKNOWLEDGMENTS

Grateful acknowledgement is made to the following publications where these poems or previous versions of them first appeared. Readers, interns, and editors—your work is deeply appreciated.

"Ash and Warm Air," "Conversation," and "Foundation" appeared in *A Chapbook of Talks and Poetry: Honoring Palestinian Poet Mahmoud Darwish* as "Shed Notes I, III, and IV."

"Appetite" appeared in *Orion Magazine*.

"Bathhouse": earlier versions appeared in *Mid-American Review* and as "Visiting Tenakee Springs, AK" in *Roanoke Review*.

"Carved on the Docks" appeared in *Reflection* as "Indian Mask Carved on the Docks."

"Exposure" as "Light Boat" and "Net Work" appeared in *Four Way Review*.

"Gracias" appeared in *Town Creek Poetry*.

"Growing Up" appeared in *The Greensboro Review*.

"Grub" appeared in *Gonzaga: The Magazine of Gonzaga University*.

"Housewarming" and "The View" appeared in *Prairie Schooner*.

"Independence Day at Rose's" appeared in *Cirque: A Literary Journal for the North Pacific Rim* as "Pelican, AK."

"Leftovers" appeared in *REAL: Regarding Arts and Letters* as "Untitled."

"Not Fishing" appeared in *Mid-American Review*.

"Playboy" appeared in *Open to Interpretation: Love + Lust* as "So What."

"Pleasure" appeared in *Mason's Road*.

"Predawn" appeared in *Connotations: The Island Institute Journal*.

"Rockfish" and "Weather Report" appeared in *The Elephants*.

"Rose's" appeared in *The Fourth River*.

"Shame" appeared in *Hawaii Pacific Review*.

"The Song of a Boat" appeared in *Valparaiso Poetry Review* as "Elegy for a Boat."

"The Sound of Oars" appeared in *Ploughshares* and was reprinted in *Rise Up Review*.

"Town Day" appeared in *Gulf Coast: A Journal of Literature and Fine Arts*.

"Triangulation" appeared in *The Seattle Review of Books*.

"Under the Madrone" [The stranger said: Love is a vise…] appeared as "Divorce" in *Crab Orchard Review*.

"Independence Day at Rose's," "Predawn," "Rose's," and "Shame" also appeared in *Anchored in Deep Water: The FisherPoets Anthology*.

Many of these poems appeared in *Aristotle's Lantern*, a chapbook from Seven Kitchens Press.

I am grateful to the Island Institute, the Sitka Center for Art and Ecology, and Hedgebrook, for the luxury of time. I am also grateful to the Elizabeth George Foundation for the practicality of two hours every day; the FisherPoets Gathering for the sense of community; and the Hugo House, where I will always keep learning.

Thank you to Bear Star Press for making a home for these poems.

Thank you to Ed Skoog for finding the title and to Marci Calabretta Cancio-Bello for helping me see the shape of the book.

Thank you to my teachers: Dorianne Laux, Joseph Millar, John Balaban, and Tod Marshall. You've become friends.

Thank you to my friends: Kari Smith, Cortney Phillips Meriwether, J. Scott Brownlee, Matthew Wimberley, Noah Lloyd, Shobha Rao, James Crews, Brendan Jones, Ashley Booth, Shelley Goldstein, Beth Kruse, Andrea Woods, Daemond Arrindell, Anastacia Renee, and my partner in all things beautiful, Brian Hagenbuch. You've become teachers.

Thank you to my parents, Jeff and Leslie Golden, who try every day to give me the world.

An ocean of gratitude and love for the people, creatures, and places that inspired this book. There aren't enough poems in the world to describe just how extraordinary you are.